i

SECRETARY OF DEFENSE ASH CARTER
SUBMITTED STATEMENT TO THE SENATE ARMED SERVICES
COMMITTEE ON THE FY 2016 BUDGET REQUEST FOR THE
DEPARTMENT OF DEFENSE
TUESDAY, MARCH 3, 2015

Chairman McCain, Ranking Member Reed, Members of the Committee: thank you for confirming me as Secretary of Defense, and for inviting me here today to discuss the President's Fiscal Year 2016 budget request for the Department of Defense (DoD). Oversight is key to our system of government. I not only welcome your wisdom and experience; I also want your partnership, and need your help.

I also want to thank Chairman Dempsey for his leadership, as well as Deputy Secretary Work and Vice Chairman Winnefeld, in particular for all their hard work over the past year in helping develop the budget request we will be discussing today.

I. INTRODUCTION AND STRATEGY

Since I last appeared before this committee, I had the opportunity to see our troops in Afghanistan and Kuwait. Hearing from them was one of my highest priorities upon taking office.

In Afghanistan, our soldiers, sailors, airmen, and Marines are helping cement progress made toward a more secure, stable, and prosperous future, by training, advising, and assisting Afghan forces and continuing their counter-terrorism mission. They are working to ensure that Afghanistan never again becomes a safe haven for attacks on our homeland, or on our partners and allies.

In Kuwait, our men and women in uniform are contributing to our counter-ISIL coalition in Iraq and Syria. They are working closely with Iraq and our global coalition partners to ensure that local forces can deliver lasting defeat to a vile enemy that has barbarically murdered American citizens, Iraqis, Syrians, and so many others, and that seeks to export its hateful and twisted ideology across the Middle East and North Africa, and beyond.

No doubt the challenges and opportunities we face extend well beyond the Middle East.

In Europe, our troops are helping reinforce and reassure our allies in Eastern Europe as we confront a reversion to archaic security thinking.

In the Asia-Pacific – home to half the world's population and economy – they are working to modernize our alliances, build new partnerships, and helping the United States continue to underwrite stability, peace, and prosperity in the region – as we have for decades.

And as we still meet longtime challenges, such as the continuing imperative to counter the spread of weapons of mass destruction, our armed forces are also addressing new dangers, such as in cyberspace.

Across the world, it is America's leadership, and America's men and women in uniform, who often stand between disorder and order – who stand up to malicious and destabilizing actors, while standing behind those who believe in a more secure, just, and prosperous future.

Mr. Chairman, this committee and this Congress will determine whether our troops can continue to do so – whether they can continue to defend our nation's interests around the world with the readiness, capability, and excellence our nation has grown accustomed to, and sometimes taken for granted.

Halting and reversing the decline in defense spending imposed by the Budget Control Act, the President's budget would give us the resources we need to execute our nation's defense strategy.

It would ensure we field a modern, ready force in a balanced way, while also embracing change and reform, because asking for more taxpayer dollars requires we hold up our end of the bargain – by ensuring that every dollar is well-spent.

The President is proposing to increase the defense budget in Fiscal Year 2016, but in line with the projection he submitted to Congress last year in the Fiscal Year 2015 budget's Future Years Defense Program (FYDP). The department is executing the plan it presented last year. Accordingly, for Fiscal Year 2016, the President is proposing $534 billion for DoD's base budget and $51 billion in Overseas Contingency Operations (OCO), totaling $585 billion to sustain America's national security and defense strategies.

The Defense Department needs your support for this budget, which is driven by strategy, not the other way around. More specifically, it is driven by the defense strategy identified in the 2014 Quadrennial Defense Review, which reflects the longtime, bipartisan consensus that our military must protect the homeland, build security globally, and project power and win decisively. We do so in line with our longstanding tradition of maintaining a superior force with an unmatched technological edge, working in close partnership with friends and allies, upholding the rules-based international order, and keeping our commitments to the people who make up the all-volunteer force.

Our defense budget's priorities line up with our strategic priorities: sustaining America's global leadership by:

- rebalancing to the Asia-Pacific region;
- maintaining a strong commitment to security and stability in Europe and the Middle East;
- sustaining a global counterterrorism campaign;
- strengthening key alliances and partnerships; and,
- prioritizing key modernization efforts.

This budget ensures we can execute our defense strategy with manageable risk, even as it does require us to accept elevated risk in some areas.

But – and I want to be clear about this – parts of our nation's defense strategy cannot be executed under sequestration, which remains the law of the land and is set to return 212 days from today.

As I have said before, the prospect of sequestration's serious damage to our national security and economy is tragically not a result of an economic emergency or recession.

It is not because these budget cuts are a mathematical solution to the nation's overall fiscal challenge – they are not.

It is not because paths of curbing nondiscretionary spending and reforming our tax system have been explored and exhausted – they have not.

It is not due to a breakthrough in military technology or a new strategic insight that somehow makes continued defense spending unnecessary – there has been no such silver bullet.

And it is not because the world has suddenly become more peaceful – for it is abundantly clear that it has not.

Instead, sequestration is purely the collateral damage of political gridlock. And friends and potential enemies around the world are watching.

We in the Department of Defense are prepared to make difficult strategic and budgetary choices. We are also committed – more than ever before – to finding new ways to improve the way we do business and be more efficient and accountable in our defense spending.

But in order to ensure our military remains the world's finest fighting force, we need to banish the clouds of fiscal uncertainty that have obscured our plans and forced inefficient choices. We need a long-term restoration of normal budgeting and a deal that the President can sign, and that lives up to our responsibility of defending this country and the global order. And that means, among other things, avoiding sequestration.

To be sure, even under sequestration, America will remain the world's strongest military power. But under sequestration, our military – and our national security – would have to take on irresponsible and unnecessary risk – risk that previous Administrations and Congressional leaders have wisely chosen to avoid.

Sequestration would lead over time to a military that looks fundamentally different and performs much differently than what we are used to. Not only as Secretary of Defense, but simply as an American, I deeply, earnestly hope we can avert that future. I am committed to working with the members of this committee, and your colleagues throughout the Congress to prevent it.

I know how proud you and all Americans are that we field the finest fighting force in the world. But our military superiority was not built, and will not be sustained, by resting on our laurels. So instead of resigning ourselves to having the diminished military that sequestration would give us, I propose that we build the force of the future, together.

II. BUILDING THE FORCE OF THE FUTURE

Assuming the Congress funds the President's Fiscal Year 2016 budget and averts sequestration, we have the opportunity to build the force of the future. We have inherited a long tradition of military excellence from those who came before us, and we must preserve it for those who will come after.

But to do so, DoD must embrace the future – and embrace change – throughout our institution. We must be open to new ideas and new ways of doing business that can help us operate more efficiently and perform more effectively in an increasingly dynamic and competitive environment.

What DoD Needs To Do

As DoD counters the very real dangers we face in the world, we will also grab hold of the bright opportunities before us – opportunities to be more competitive and re-forge our nation's military and defense establishment into a future force that harnesses and develops the latest, cutting-edge technology, and that remains superior to any potential adversary; one that is efficient and accountable to the taxpayers who support it; and one that competes and succeeds in attracting the next generation of talented Americans to fill its ranks.

These are the three main pillars on which DoD will build the force of the future.

Competitiveness through Technological and Operational Superiority

As other nations pursue comprehensive military modernization programs and develop technologies designed to blunt our military's traditional advantages, the first pillar of our future force must be ensuring that we maintain – and extend – our technological edge over any potential adversary.

The President's Fiscal Year 2016 budget includes targeted investments in modernized space, cyber, and missile defense capabilities geared toward countering emerging threats that could upend our technological superiority and our ability to project power. DoD would look forward to providing a full account of our proposed modernization investments, and the threats that compel them, in a classified setting.

The budget also supports the Defense Innovation Initiative, which will help ensure the military continues to ride the leading edge of innovation, and makes deferred modernization investments that will ensure America's nuclear deterrent remains safe, secure, and effective. Across all these efforts, we must be open to global, commercial technology as well, and learn from advances in the private sector.

Because we know that technology alone – however advanced – cannot sustain our military's superiority, just as important is a ruthless focus on operational excellence. This means using our existing forces and capabilities in new, creative, and fiscally prudent ways to achieve our objectives. This also means working to develop more innovative and effective strategic and military options for the President, introducing a new and more rapidly responsive global force management model, developing new operational concepts, and reforming and updating all our operational plans.

Competitiveness through Accountability & Efficiency

The second pillar of building the force of the future requires redoubling our efforts to make DoD more accountable and efficient. We live in a competitive world and need to be a competitive organization. If we don't lean ourselves out and maintain our fighting weight, we have no business asking our fellow citizens for more resources.

As I made clear in my confirmation hearing, I cannot suggest greater support and stability for the defense budget without at the same time frankly noting that not every defense dollar is always spent as well as it should be.

American taxpayers rightly have trouble comprehending – let alone supporting – the defense budget when they read of cost overruns, lack of accounting and accountability, needless overhead, and the like.

If we're asking taxpayers to not only give us half a trillion of their hard-earned dollars, but also give us more than we got last year, we have to demonstrate that we can be responsible with it.

We must do all we can to spend their money more wisely and more responsibly. We must reduce overhead, and we must curb wasteful spending practices wherever they are.

DoD has sought to continuously improve our acquisition processes over the past five years, and I am proud myself to have been a part of that effort. Today, I am recommitting the Defense Department to working both with Congress, and on our own, to find new and more creative ways of stretching our defense dollars to give our troops the weapons and equipment they need.

The department's Better Buying Power initiative is now on its third iteration since I established it in 2010, with Better Buying Power 3.0 focused on achieving dominant capabilities through technical excellence. I know well and very much appreciate the strong support for acquisition reform demonstrated by the Senate and House Armed Services Committees, and their

Chairmen, and I share their deep desire to achieve real, lasting results that benefit both America's security and taxpayers.

DoD is working closely with committee Members and staff on ways to eliminate some of the burdensome and duplicative administrative requirements levied on our program managers. To that end, the President's FY 2016 budget submission includes a number of legislative proposals designed to help streamline the program oversight process. We look forward to continuing our close partnership with Congress to see these measures implemented.

As we sustain our focus on acquisition reform, I believe that DoD must concurrently undertake a wholesale review of our business practices and management systems.

Our goal is to identify where we can further reduce the cost of doing business to free up funding for readiness and modernization – ensuring that our energy, focus, and resources are devoted to supporting our frontline operations as much as possible.

We intend to work closely with industry partners – who execute or enable many of our programs, logistics, training, administrative, and other functions – throughout this process, both to explore how they could help us accomplish our missions at reduced cost, and because they may have new and innovative ideas worth considering.

Additionally, the Defense Department is pursuing creative force structure changes to be more agile and efficient – such as how we're modernizing our cruisers and restructuring Army aviation. We've established a new Defense POW/MIA Accounting Agency. And four previous rounds of efficiency and budget reduction initiatives have yielded approximately $78 billion in projected and actual savings in FY 2016, helping to cushion our defense programs from successive years of budget cuts.

We're also working hard to cut unnecessary overhead: from reducing management headquarters budgets by 20 percent across the department, to divesting excess bases and infrastructure.

When DoD recently requested a round of domestic Base Realignment and Closure, Congress asked that we first pursue efficiencies in Europe. We did. DoD has approved and is pursuing a broad European Infrastructure Consolidation – which will result in some $500 million in annual recurring savings. We now need a round of domestic BRAC beginning in Fiscal Year 2017 to address excess infrastructure here at home.

Simply put, we have more bases in more places than we need. We estimate DoD has about 25 percent more infrastructure capacity than necessary. We must be permitted to divest surplus infrastructure as we reduce and renew force structure. With projected recurring savings from a new BRAC round totaling some $2 billion a year, it would be irresponsible to cut tooth without also cutting tail.

For base communities in question, it's important to remember that BRAC is often an opportunity to be seized. Communities have shown that BRAC is ultimately what you make of it, and there are plenty of places that have emerged from it stronger than they were before.

Consider Lawrence, Indiana, which took advantage of Fort Harrison's closure in 1996 to create an enterprise zone, community college, recreational facilities, and commercial sites that in just 7 years not only replaced 100 percent of the jobs lost when the base closed, but created even more.

Charleston, South Carolina stepped up when the Charleston Naval Complex closed in 1993, and now is home to more than 80 new industrial and federal agency tenants. The former naval base is now producing millions of dollars' worth of goods that are exported to Europe, Africa, and the Middle East.

And at former Mather Air Force Base in Sacramento County, California, the local redevelopment effort has invested $400 million and created more than 6,500 jobs – over six times the number of jobs lost when the base closed in 1993. It's now home to scores of businesses, a mixture of private companies, government agencies, and non-profit organizations.

These are just a few examples of what can happen when local leaders, communities, and businesses work together and take advantage of the opportunities for new jobs and new growth after BRAC.

One more point on accountability: Whether we're improving acquisition or closing bases, it is not enough to simply tell taxpayers that we're spending their dollars responsibly. We have to also show them, which is why good cost accounting and financial auditability is so important to me.

DoD has made significant progress over the past five years in adding more discipline to our business environment, but there is much work left to be done, and we remain fully committed to our current audit goals.

Today, over 90 percent of DoD's current year, general fund budgetary resources are under some form of financial audit, with the military services all involved and following the model employed by the Marine Corps.

We plan to submit every corner of DoD to this kind of audit regimen beginning in FY 2016. With this foundation, the department will progressively expand the scope of these audits until all our organizations, funds, and financial statements will be under audit in FY 2018, complying with Congress's statutory direction to be audit ready by the end of FY 2017.

There's a reason why auditing is a basic practice as ancient as the Domesday Book, and it is time that DoD finally lives up to its moral and legal obligation to be accountable to those who pay its bills. I intend to do everything we can – including holding people to account – to get this done.

Competitiveness through Attracting Future Talent

Third, but no less important, DoD must be competitive when it comes to attracting new generations of talented and dedicated Americans to our calling of defending the nation.

We know how the attacks of September 11th, 2001 motivated so many Americans to want to be part of this noble endeavor. Going forward, we must ensure our future force can continue to recruit the finest young men and women our country has to offer – military and civilian – like those who serve today.

As we do this, we must be mindful that the next generation expects jobs that give them purpose, meaning, and dignity. They want to be able to make real contributions, have their voices heard, and gain valuable and transferable experience. We must shape the kind of force they want to be in. The battle for talent will demand enlightened and agile leaders, new training schemes, new educational opportunities, and new compensation approaches.

DoD is already pursuing several initiatives that will help ensure the military is a compelling career option. In recent years, we've been expanding pilot programs that facilitate breaks in service that let our people gain diverse work experience. We've tailored our transition assistance program, Transition GPS, to better prepare servicemembers to enter the civilian workforce – providing different tracks for those who want to go to college, those who want skills training, and those who want to be entrepreneurs. And we've put a renewed focus on military ethics and professionalism, as well as making sure our military health system is held to the same high-quality standards we expect from the servicemembers and military family members under its care.

Because we know how important it is – both for today's servicemembers and the generation that will follow them – we're also deeply committed to creating an environment and culture where we live the values we defend and every servicemember is treated with the dignity and respect they deserve.

That's why we're continuing to expand combat positions available to women – because everyone who's able and willing to serve their country should have full and equal opportunity to do so.

It's why we're striving to eliminate sexual assault from the military.

And it's why we've been making sure gay and lesbian servicemembers can serve openly, and that their families receive the benefits their loved ones have earned.

But for everything we're doing, DoD cannot build the force of the future by ourselves. We need Congress's help.

What We Need Congress To Do

Since our current defense budget drawdown began several years ago, I've observed something of a phenomenon here in Washington.

Along with our troops, their families, and our defense civilians, I thank our supporters on Capitol Hill, including most members of this committee, who have joined with us in trying to do everything possible to get Congress to prevent more mindless cuts to our defense budget.

Unfortunately, these combined efforts have been unsuccessful in actually restoring adequate and predictable resources for DoD. We have had to endure deep cuts to readiness, weather pay freezes and civilian furloughs, and cut badly needed investments in modernization and critical technologies. At the same time, Congress has sometimes sought to protect programs that DoD has argued are no longer needed, or require significant reform.

We have had the worst of both worlds – a double whammy of mindless sequestration coupled with inability to reform.

As many of you know, it wasn't always this way.

During the defense drawdown after the Cold War, DoD had much more flexibility thanks to the help of Congress. For example, we were able to resize the Army, retire the A-6 Intruder and many other weapons systems, and implement multiple BRAC rounds, which freed up dollars we re-allocated to keep our force structure ready, capable, and deployable around the world.

I know some of the changes and reforms we're proposing may feel like a significant change from how we currently do business. But if anyone can understand how the dots connect and how we need Congress's help to be able to defend our country, our allies, and our interests in an increasingly dangerous world, it's you – the members of this committee.

The fact is, if we're not able to implement the changes and reforms we need, we will be forced to make painful tradeoffs, even at the higher topline the President is requesting. We will lose further ground on modernization and readiness – leaving tomorrow's force less capable and leaving our nation less secure. And we will face significant hurdles to executing our nation's defense strategy. That's why we need your help.

III. THE PRESIDENT'S FISCAL YEAR 2016 BUDGET

As we do every year when formulating our budget, this budget seeks to balance readiness, capability, and size – because we must ensure that, whatever the size of our force, we have the resources to provide every servicemember with the right training, the right equipment, the right compensation, and the right quality of fellow troops. That is the only way we can ensure our military is fully prepared to accomplish its missions.

Almost two-thirds of DoD's Fiscal Year 2016 base budget – $348.4 billion – funds our day-to-day expenses, similar to what a business would call its operating budget. This covers, among other expenses, the cost of fuel, spare parts, logistics support, maintenance, service contracts, and administration. It also includes pay and benefits for military and civilian personnel, which by themselves comprise nearly half of our total budget.

The remaining third of our base budget – $185.9 billion – comprises investments in future defense needs, much like a business' capital improvement budget. It pays for the research, development, testing, evaluation, and ultimately acquisition of the weapons, equipment, and facilities that our servicemembers need.

Broken down differently, our base budget includes the following categories:

- Military pay and benefits (including health care and retirement benefits) – $169 billion, or about 32 percent of the base budget.
- Civilian pay and benefits – $79 billion, or about 15 percent of the base budget.
- Other operating costs – $105 billion, or about 20 percent of the base budget.
- Acquisition and other investments (Procurement; research, development, testing, and evaluation; and new facilities construction) – $181 billion, or about 34 percent of the base budget.

Modernization

What makes this budget different is the focus it puts, more so than any other over the last decade, on new funding for modernization. After years of war, which required the deferral of longer-term modernization investments, this budget puts renewed emphasis on preparing for future threats – especially threats that challenge our military's power projection capabilities.

Threats to Power Projection and our Technological Edge

Being able to project power anywhere across the globe by rapidly surging aircraft, ships, troops, and supplies lies at the core of our defense strategy and what the American people have come to expect of their military. It guarantees that when an acute crisis erupts anywhere in the world, America can provide aid when disaster strikes, reinforce our allies when they are threatened, and protect our citizens and interests globally. It also assures freedom of navigation and overflight, and allows global commerce to flow freely.

For decades, U.S. global power projection has relied on the ships, planes, submarines, bases, aircraft carriers, satellites, networks, and other advanced capabilities that comprise our military's unrivaled technological edge. But today that superiority is being challenged in unprecedented ways.

Advanced military technologies, from rockets and drones to chemical and biological capabilities, have found their way into the arsenals of both non-state actors as well as previously less capable militaries. And other nations – among them Russia, China, Iran, and North Korea – have been pursuing long-term, comprehensive military modernization programs to close the technology gap that has long existed between them and the United States.

These modernization programs are developing and fielding advanced aircraft, submarines, and both longer-range and more accurate ballistic and cruise missiles. They're developing new and advanced anti-ship and anti-air missiles, as well as new counter-space, cyber, electronic warfare, undersea, and air attack capabilities. In some areas, we see levels of new weapons development that we haven't seen since the mid-1980s, near the peak of the Soviet Union's surge in Cold War defense spending.

Targeted Investments in the President's Budget

One of the reasons we are asking for more money this year than last year is to reverse recent under-investment in new weapons systems by making targeted investments to help us stay ahead of emerging threats – adding substantial funding for space control and launch capabilities, missile defense, cyber, and advanced sensors, communications, and munitions – all of which are critical for power projection in contested environments.

The budget also makes significant investments in the resilience and survivability of our infrastructure and forces, particularly in the western Pacific, with improved active defenses such as our Patriot and AEGIS systems, as well as selective hardening of key installations and facilities.

DoD is also addressing the erosion of U.S. technological superiority with the Defense Innovation Initiative (DII). The DII is an ambitious department-wide effort to identify and invest in innovative ways to sustain and advance America's military dominance for the 21st century.

The DII will identify, develop, and field breakthrough technologies and systems through a new Long-Range Research & Development Planning Program, and the President's budget supports this effort through specific investments in promising new technologies and capabilities such as high-speed strike weapons, advanced aeronautics, rail guns, and high energy lasers. The DII also involves the development of innovative operational concepts that would help us use our current capabilities in new and creative ways. The ultimate aim is to help craft 'offset strategies' that maximize our strengths and exploit the weaknesses of potential adversaries.

Our budget is also making focused and sustained investments in modernization and manning across the nuclear enterprise, even as we reduce the roles and numbers of nuclear weapons in the U.S. nuclear posture. These investments are critical for ensuring the continued safety, security, and effectiveness of our nuclear deterrent, as well as the long-term health of the force that supports our nuclear triad, particularly after recent troubling lapses in parts of DoD's nuclear enterprise. To help fund improvements across the nuclear enterprise, we are requesting an increase of approximately $1 billion in Fiscal Year 2016, and about $8 billion over the FYDP.

Readiness

DoD must rebuild and recover after more than 13 years of uninterrupted war. But our effort to do so has been frustrated by two variables, both of which are out of our hands – one, the continued high operational tempo and high demand for our forces, and two, the uncertainty surrounding annual appropriations.

Only over the last couple of years has readiness begun to recover from the strains of over a decade of war, exacerbated by sequestration in 2013. Nevertheless, readiness remains at troubling levels across the force.

While our forward-deployed forces remain ready, our surge forces at home are not as ready as they need to be. The President's budget therefore invests in near-term unit readiness by adjusting service end-strength ramps to reduce personnel turbulence and stress on the force, while increasing funding to improve home station training and training-related infrastructure.

This past year has demonstrated that our military must be ready to fight more than just the last war. We have to be prepared across all domains – air, land, sea, space, and in cyberspace – to engage in both low- and high-end missions and conflicts, as well as in the shadowy, so-called 'hybrid warfare' space in between.

While this budget submission's requested and projected funding levels will enable the military to continue making steady progress toward full-spectrum combat readiness, the gains we've recently made are fragile. Sustaining them to provide for ready and capable forces will require both time and a stable flow of resources, which is why, even under the budget we're requesting, the Army, Navy, and Marine Corps won't all reach their readiness goals until 2020, and the Air Force won't do so until 2023.

Army:

For Fiscal Year 2016, the Army's base budget of $126.5 billion supports an end-strength of 1,015,000 soldiers – 475,000 soldiers on active duty, 342,000 soldiers in the Army National Guard, and 198,000 soldiers in the Army Reserve – comprising 57 total force brigade combat teams and associated enablers. The budget also supports 19 brigade-level training rotations at the Army's Combat Training Centers, which are critical to the Army's efforts to reach full-spectrum combat readiness.

While the Army's postwar end-strength target remains a force of approximately 450,000 active-duty soldiers, 335,000 Army National Guard soldiers and 195,000 Army Reserve soldiers, this year's budget slows the drawdown rate. Rather than planning to reduce the active-duty force by 20,000 soldiers and the National Guard by 14,000 soldiers in Fiscal Year 2016, the Army will instead plan to reduce by 15,000 active-duty soldiers and 8,000 Guardsmen, while still maintaining its schedule for reducing unit structure. This will help mitigate personnel turbulence and stress, while also improving unit manning as the Army approaches its target size.

The Army's budget for Fiscal Year 2016 also includes $4.5 billion for Army helicopter modernization. Specifically:

- UH-60M Black Hawk: We are requesting $1.6 billion to support buying 94 multi-mission helicopters in FY 2016, and $6.1 billion for 301 helicopters over the FYDP.
- AH-64E Apache: We are requesting $1.4 billion to support development and purchase of 64 attack helicopters in FY 2016, and $6.2 billion for 303 helicopters over the FYDP.
- CH-47F Chinook: We are requesting $1.1 billion to support development and purchase of 39 cargo helicopters in FY 2016, and $3.2 billion for 95 helicopters over the FYDP.
- UH-72 Lakota: We are requesting $187 million in FY 2016 to support the final buy of 28 light utility helicopters.

These investments require difficult trade-offs given today's constrained fiscal environment. That is why the Army is resubmitting the Army's Aviation Restructure Initiative, which makes the most efficient use of taxpayer dollars by retiring outdated airframes and streamlining the Army's helicopter fleet so that platforms can be modernized and allocated where they are needed most.

As you know, I am committed to reviewing the Army's Aviation Restructure Initiative. However, the Army believes that fully implementing the Aviation Restructure Initiative (ARI), which includes shifting National Guard Apaches to active-duty units while providing Guard units with Black Hawks, is prudent for several reasons.

For one, Apaches are in high demand at high levels of readiness that would require Guard units manning them to mobilize at unprecedentedly high rates; or alternatively, for the Army to spend a total of approximately $4.4 billion to fully equip the Guard's Apache battalions, and then $350 million per year to maintain them at those high levels of readiness. Meanwhile, Black Hawks are more suitable for Guard missions here at home. Whether homeland defense, disaster relief, support to civil authorities, or complementing our active-duty military, these missions tend to demand transport and medical capabilities more than the attack capabilities of Apaches. In sum, the initiative avoids approximately $12 billion in costs through Fiscal Year 2035 and saves over $1 billion annually starting in Fiscal Year 2020. Considering these figures, implementing the Aviation Restructure Initiative is not only in the best warfighting interest of the Army, but also in the interest of the taxpayers who fund it.

I know this is a contentious issue. However, we believe the ARI is the least cost, best solution for the Army's aviation enterprise. DoD looks forward to making its case to the National Commission on the Future of the Army established by the 2015 National Defense Authorization Act.

Navy & Marine Corps:

The Navy and Marine Corps are allocated $161 billion for Fiscal Year 2016, supporting a 282-ship fleet in 2016 and a 304-ship fleet by Fiscal Year 2020 with a return to 11 aircraft carriers, 386,600 active-duty and Reserve sailors, and 222,900 active-duty and Reserve Marines.

The President's budget invests $16.6 billion in shipbuilding for Fiscal Year 2016, and $95.9 billion over the FYDP. The budget protects critical Navy and Marine Corps investments in undersea, surface, amphibious, and airborne capabilities – all of which are critical for addressing emerging threats. Specifically:

- Submarines: We are requesting $5.7 billion for FY 2016, and $30.9 billion over the FYDP, to support buying two Virginia-class attack submarines a year through FY 2020. We are also requesting $1.4 billion in FY 2016, and $10.5 billion over the FYDP, to support the replacement for the Ohio-class ballistic missile submarine.
- DDG-51 Guided Missile Destroyers: We are requesting $3.4 billion for FY 2016, and $18.5 billion over the FYDP, to support the continued development and procurement of two DDG-51 destroyers a year through FY 2020.
- Aircraft Carriers: The President's budget plan enables us to support 11 carrier strike groups. We are requesting $678 million in FY 2016, and $3.9 billion over the FYDP, to support the refueling and overhaul of the U.S.S. *George Washington*. We are also requesting $2.8 billion in FY 2016, and $12.5 billion over the FYDP, to support completion of the *Gerald Ford*, fourth-year construction of the *John F. Kennedy*, and long-lead items for CVN-80, *Enterprise*.
- Littoral Combat Ships (LCS) and Small Surface Combatants: We are requesting $1.8

billion in FY 2016, and $9.4 billion over the FYDP, to support development and procurement of 14 littoral combat ships over the FYDP – including three LCS in FY 2016. We are also requesting $55 million in FY 2016, and $762.8 million over the FYDP, to support capability improvements to the survivability and lethality of the LCS required for the Navy to modify it into a small surface combatant.

- Fleet Replenishment Oiler: We are requesting $674 million to support buying one new fleet replenishment oiler, the TAO(X), in FY 2016 – part of a $2.4 billion request to buy four of them over the FYDP.
- Amphibious Transport Docks: We are requesting $668 million in FY 2016 to finish buying one San Antonio-class amphibious transport dock.
- F-35 Lightning II Joint Strike Fighter: The Department of the Navy is procuring two F-35 variants, the Navy carrier-based F-35C and the Marine Corps short-take-off-and-vertical-landing F-35B. The Navy and Marine Corps are requesting $3.1 billion in FY 2016 to support procurement of 13 aircraft – nine F-35Bs and four F-35Cs – and aircraft modifications and initial spares, and $20.9 billion over the FYDP to support procurement of 121 aircraft and aircraft modifications and initial spares.
- Patrol and Airborne Early Warning Aircraft: We are requesting $3.4 billion in FY 2016, and $10.1 billion over the FYDP, to support continued development and procurement of 47 P-8A Poseidon maritime patrol aircraft through FY 2020. We are also requesting $1.3 billion in FY 2016, and $6.1 billion over the FYDP, to support buying 24 E-2D Hawkeye airborne early warning aircraft through FY 2020.

Making these investments while also abiding by fiscal prudence, we had to make more difficult trade-offs. For that reason, we are resubmitting our request to place some of the Navy's cruisers and an amphibious landing ship – 12 ships in total, including 11 cruisers – into a phased modernization program that will provide them with enhanced capability and a longer lifespan. Given that our cruisers are the most capable ships for controlling the air defenses of a carrier strike group, and in light of anti-ship missile capabilities being pursued by other nations, this modernization program will, over the next decade and a half, be a baseline requirement for sustaining both our cruiser fleet and 11 carrier strike groups through 2045.

I acknowledge and appreciate the plan put forward in the 2015 National Defense Authorization Act, which helps us get to our goal, and which we have begun to implement. However, this plan is more expensive, and results in shorter ship life. Considering that our plan is critical for our power projection capabilities, we believe it should be implemented in full, and look forward to working with the Congress as we move forward.

Air Force:

The Air Force is allocated a base budget of $152.9 billion for Fiscal Year 2016, supporting a force of 491,700 active-duty, Guard, and Reserve airmen, 49 tactical fighter squadrons, 96 operational bombers out of a total 154-aircraft bomber fleet, and a safe, secure, and effective nuclear deterrent that includes 450 intercontinental ballistic missiles.

The Air Force's budget reflects DoD's decision to protect modernization funding for advanced capabilities and platforms most relevant to both present and emerging threats – in this case, fifth-generation fighters, long-range bombers, and mid-air refueling aircraft to assure our air superiority and global reach; both manned and remotely-piloted aircraft to help meet Combatant Commanders' needs for intelligence, surveillance, and reconnaissance (ISR); and research and development to ensure continued and competitive space launch capabilities. Specifically:

- **F-35A Lightning II Joint Strike Fighter**: We are requesting $6 billion to support buying 44 aircraft, aircraft modifications, and initial spares in FY 2016, and $33.5 billion to support buying 275 aircraft, modifications, and spares over the FYDP.
- **KC-46A Pegasus Refueling Tanker**: We are requesting $2.4 billion to buy 12 aircraft in FY 2016, and $14.6 billion to buy 72 aircraft over the FYDP.
- **Long-Range Strike Bomber**: We are requesting $1.2 billion for research and development in FY 2016, and $13.9 billion over the FYDP.
- **Remotely-Piloted Aircraft**: We are requesting $904 million to support buying 29 MQ-9A Reapers in FY 2016, and $4.8 billion to support buying 77 of them over the FYDP. This investment is critical to ensuring the Air Force has enough around-the-clock permissive ISR combat air patrols – in this case, allowing us to increase from 55 to 60 – to meet increased battlefield demands.
- **Competitive Space Launch**: This budget supports year-over-year increases in competitive space launches – going up from two in FY 2015 to three in FY 2016, and further increasing to four competitive launches in FY 2017. The budget also supports investments to mitigate DoD reliance on the RD-180 space engine that powers the Atlas V Evolved Expendable Launch Vehicle rockets.
- **Combat Rescue Helicopter**: We are requesting $156 million in FY 2016 for the Air Force's next-generation combat rescue helicopter – part of a total $1.6 billion request over the FYDP for research, development, testing, and evaluation – and requesting $717 million over the FYDP for procurement.

In light of high demand coupled with Congressional consultations, the Air Force budget reflects DoD's decision to slow the retirement timelines for three key ISR and battle management platforms.

We chose to defer the retirement of the U-2 Dragon Lady reconnaissance aircraft until Fiscal Year 2019, when planned sensor upgrades to the RQ-4 Global Hawk will combine with other capabilities to mitigate the loss of the U-2. We chose to delay the previously planned retirement of seven E-3 Sentry AWACS until Fiscal Year 2019, so they can support air operations over Iraq and Syria. And we chose to delay retirement of any E-8 JSTARS through Fiscal Year 2020, pending final approval of the Air Force's acquisition strategy for its replacement.

The Air Force budget also supports a timeline that would phase out and retire the A-10 in Fiscal Year 2019. With the gradual retirement of the A-10 that we're proposing, the Air Force will better support legacy fleet readiness and the planned schedule for standing up the F-35A by filling in some of the overall fighter maintenance personnel shortfalls with trained and qualified personnel from the retiring A-10 squadrons.

As you know, F-35 maintainer demand has already required the Air Force to use the authority Congress provided last year to move some A-10s into back-up aircraft inventory status. I should note that the Air Force is doing so only to the extent that it absolutely must, and so far intends to move far fewer A-10s into this status than what Congress has authorized. I know this is an important issue, and DoD looks forward to working with you on it.

Defense-Wide:

The remaining share of our base budget – about $94 billion – is allocated across the Department of Defense. This includes funding for cyber, U.S. Special Operations Command, the Defense Advanced Research Projects Agency, the Defense Health Agency, the Joint Staff, the Office of the Secretary of Defense, and missile defense.

For Fiscal Year 2016, a $9.6 billion total investment in missile defense helps protect the U.S. homeland, deployed forces, and our allies and partners. This includes $8.1 billion for the Missile Defense Agency, $1.6 billion of which will help ensure the reliability of U.S. ground-based interceptors, which are currently sited at Fort Greely, Alaska and Vandenberg Air Force Base, California. The budget also continues to support the President's timeline for implementing the European Phased Adaptive Approach.

Overseas Contingency Operations:

Separate from DoD's base budget, we are also requesting $50.9 billion in Overseas Contingency Operations (OCO) funding for Fiscal Year 2016. This represents a 21 percent decrease from last year's $64.2 billion in OCO funding, continuing OCO's decline since 2010, while also reflecting continued operational demands on U.S. forces around the world. OCO comprises funding for:

- Afghanistan and Other Operations: We are requesting $42.5 billion to support Operation Freedom's Sentinel and other missions. This includes $7.8 billion for reset and retrograde of U.S. equipment from Afghanistan, as well as $3.8 billion for training and equipping the Afghan National Security Forces through our ongoing train-advise-and-assist mission.
- Counter-ISIL Operations: We are requesting $5.3 billion to support Operation Inherent Resolve. This includes $1.3 billion for training and equipping Iraqi forces, including Kurdish forces, and the vetted moderate Syrian opposition.
- Counterterrorism Partnerships Fund: Reflecting the vital role that our allies and partners play in countering terrorism that could threaten U.S. citizens, we are requesting $2.1 billion for the Counterterrorism Partnerships Fund that President Obama established last year.
- NATO Reassurance: We are requesting $789 million for the European Reassurance Initiative, which the President created last year to help reassure our NATO allies and reinforce our Article V commitment in light of Russia's violations of Ukrainian sovereignty.

The conclusion of major combat operations in Afghanistan and Iraq has resulted in a 73 percent drop in DoD's OCO costs from their $187-billion peak in Fiscal Year 2008.

We are continuing to use OCO as appropriate to finance our military's response to unforeseen crises, but we must also account for those enduring priorities that we do not envision going away – such as supporting our Afghan partners, countering terrorism, maintaining a strong forward presence in the Middle East, and ensuring our military is ready to respond to a wide range of potential crises.

The Administration intends to transition OCO's enduring costs to the base budget between Fiscal Years 2017 and 2020. We will do this over time, and in a way that protects our defense strategy – including DoD's abilities to deter aggression, maintain crisis-ready forces, and project power across the globe. This transition, however, will not be possible unless the threat of sequestration has been removed.

Having financed the costs of key military activities – such as counterterrorism operations and our Middle East posture – outside the base budget for 14 years, and knowing that the security situation in the Middle East remains volatile, it will take time to determine which OCO costs are most likely to be enduring, and which are not. But we will release a plan later this year, which will also address how we will budget for uncertainty surrounding unforeseen future crises, and implications for DoD's budget.

IV. COMPENSATION

The choices we face about military compensation are vexing, critically important, and closely followed, so I want to be direct and upfront with you.

When our troops go into battle – risking their lives – we owe to them, and their families, not only adequate pay and compensation, but also the right investments – in the right people, the right training, and the right weapons and equipment – so that they can accomplish their missions and come home safely.

To meet all of these obligations at once, we have to balance how we allocate our dollars. It would be irresponsible to prioritize compensation, force size, equipment, or training in isolation, only to put our servicemembers' lives at unacceptable risk in battle.

For the President's Fiscal Year 2016 budget, the Defense Department considered its compensation proposals very carefully, as well as those approved by Congress in the 2015 National Defense Authorization Act. Accordingly, this budget again proposes modest adjustments to shift funds from compensation into readiness, capability, and force structure, so that our people can continue executing their missions with continued excellence.

As you know, the Congressionally-commissioned Military Compensation and Retirement Modernization Commission has recently released its own compensation proposals. Their work, which DoD is continuing to analyze, shows thoughtfulness and good intent, which we deeply appreciate.

Given that this hearing is being held before the department has submitted its recommendations on the commission's report to President Obama, it would not be appropriate for me to discuss them at this time. Many of these proposals would significantly affect our servicemembers and their families, and DoD owes them, the President, and the country our utmost diligence and most rigorous analysis.

However, I can say that the department agrees with the overarching goals of the commission, especially providing servicemembers and beneficiaries more options – whether in preparing for retirement or in making health care choices.

I can also say that the commission's proposals are complicated, and do not lend themselves to binary answers. Therefore, when we provide the President with our recommendations on each proposal, DoD will clarify not simply whether we support each proposal, but also where we recommend specific modifications to improve or enable us to fully support a given proposal.

We believe there is something positive in almost every one of the commission's recommendations, and that they present a great opportunity to ensure we honor our servicemembers past, present, and future. I look forward to Congress's support and partnership as we work hard to take advantage of it.

V. IMPACT OF SEQUESTRATION

At the end of 2013, policymakers came together on a bipartisan basis to partially reverse sequestration and pay for higher discretionary funding levels with long-term reforms. We've seen how that bipartisan agreement has allowed us to invest in areas ranging from research and manufacturing to strengthening our military. We've also seen the positive impact on our economy, with a more responsible and orderly budget process helping contribute to the fastest job growth since the late 1990s.

The President's budget builds on this progress by reversing sequestration, paid for with a balanced mix of commonsense spending cuts and tax loophole closures, while also proposing additional deficit reduction that would put debt on a downward path as a share of the economy. The President has also made clear that he will not accept a budget that locks in sequestration going forward.

As the Joint Chiefs and others have outlined, and as I will detail in this testimony, sequestration would damage our national security, ultimately resulting in a military that is too small and insufficiently equipped to fully implement our defense strategy. This would reflect poorly on America's global leadership, which has been the one critical but defining constant in a turbulent and dangerous world. In fact, even the threat of sequestration has had real effects.

You don't need me to tell you that the President has said he will not accept a budget that severs the vital link between our national and economic security. Why? Because the strength of our nation depends on the strength of our economy, and a strong military depends on a strong educational system, thriving private-sector businesses, and innovative research. And because that principle – matching defense increases with non-defense increases dollar-for-dollar – was a basic condition of the bipartisan agreement we got in 2013. The President sees no reason why we shouldn't uphold those same principles in any agreement now.

The only way we're going to get out of the wilderness of sequestration is if we work together. I therefore appeal to members of Congress, from both parties, to start looking for ways to find a truly bipartisan compromise. I hope they can make clear to their colleagues that sequestration would also damage America's long-term strength, preventing our country from making pro-growth investments in areas ranging from basic research to early childhood education – investments that, in the past, have helped make our military the finest fighting force the world has ever known.

Sequestration is set to return in just over 200 days. Letting that happen would be unwise and unsafe for our national defense, over both the short and long term.

Short-Term Impact

DoD has had to live with uncertain budgets for the last three years, continuous and sudden downward revisions of our budget plans, and even a government closure. To continue meeting all of our mission requirements, we've done our best to manage through these circumstances, underfunding significant parts of our force and its support systems. Put bluntly, we have survived, but not thrived. Our military has made painful choices and tradeoffs among the size, capabilities, and readiness of our joint force, and we've amassed a number of bills that are now coming due.

That's why the department has been counting on and planning for a budget increase of roughly $35 billion above sequestration-level caps in Fiscal Year 2016. If it looks like DoD will be operating at sequestration levels in 2016, on October 1 we will have to swiftly begin making cuts so that we don't end up $35 billion short as we approach year's end.

A return to sequestration in Fiscal Year 2016 would affect all aspects of the department, but not all equally.

More than one-third of the Fiscal Year 2016 cuts would come have to come from Operations and Maintenance accounts, with unavoidable reductions in readiness and our ability to shape world events in America's interest. Let me put this more plainly: allowing sequestration to return would deprive our troops of what they need to accomplish their missions.

Approximately half of the cuts would have to come from the department's modernization accounts, undermining our efforts to secure technological superiority for U.S. forces in future conflicts. Because there are bills that DoD absolutely must pay – such as the salaries of our troops – many capabilities being developed to counter known threats from highly capable adversaries would be delayed or cancelled, deepening our nation's vulnerabilities at a time when the world is growing more dangerous, not less. Sequestration would put a hold on critical programs like our Aerospace Innovation Initiative, the Next Generation Adaptive Engine, the Ground-Based Interceptor missile defense kill vehicle redesign, and several space control efforts.

Deferring these investments is bad policy and makes the Defense Department less competitive for the future. What's more, it breaks faith with the troops of today and the troops of tomorrow. And it undermines the defense industrial base that is a critical foundation for our national security.

Long-Term Impact

If sequestration were to persist over time, the long-term consequences would be harder hitting. We would ultimately have a military that looks fundamentally different, and that performs much differently, from what our nation is accustomed to.

If we are forced to sequestration-level budgets, I do not believe that we can continue to make incremental cuts and maintain the same general set of objectives as we've had in our defense strategy. I will insist that new cuts be accompanied by a frank reassessment of our strategic approach to addressing the threats we face around the world – what we are asking the Armed Forces to do and to be prepared to do.

I cannot tell you right now exactly what that means – DoD is not resigned to the return of sequestration – but I can tell you that I will direct the department to look at all aspects of the defense budget to determine how best to absorb these cuts. No portion of our budget can remain inviolate.

What I will not do is let DoD continue mortgaging our future readiness and capability. I will not send our troops into a fight with outdated equipment, inadequate readiness, and ineffective doctrine.

Everything else is on the table.

What does that mean? We could be forced to consider pay cuts, not just cuts in the growth of compensation. We could be forced to consider all means of shedding excess infrastructure, not just working within the Congressional BRAC process. We could be forced to look at significant force structure cuts, not just trimming around the edges. We could be forced to ask our military to do – and be prepared to do – significantly less than what we have traditionally expected, and required of it.

I am not afraid to ask these difficult questions, but if we are stuck with sequestration's budget cuts over the long term, our entire nation will have to live with the answers.

A prolonged period of depressed defense budgets will almost certainly mean a smaller, less capable, and less ready military. No one can fully predict the impact on the future. But it could translate into future conflicts that last longer, and are more costly in both lives and dollars.

That may sound severe to some, but it is a fact, and history should be our guide when we think about the true cost of sequestration.

The Case for Repealing Sequestration

I know I'm preaching to the choir here. If sequestration could have been reversed by just this committee and its counterpart in the House, it probably would have happened years ago. So I offer the following to Members of the Committee about what you can remind your colleagues when you ask for their vote to repeal sequestration:

Remind them that even after the increase we're asking for, DoD's budget as a share of total federal spending will still be at a near-historic low – a quarter of what it was during the Korean War, a third of what it was during the Vietnam War, and half of what it was during the Reagan buildup.

Remind them that the increased funding is for modernization that's critical to keeping our military's technological edge and staying ahead of potential adversaries.

Remind them that DoD has hands-on leadership from the very top – me – devoted to using taxpayer dollars better than they've been used in the past. You have my personal commitment to greater accountability, greater efficiency, and running this department better and leaner than before.

Remind them that sequestration's cuts to long-term investments will likely make those investments more costly down the line. All who bemoan unnecessary Pentagon program delays and the associated cost overruns should know that sequestration will only make these problems worse. I can easily sympathize with my non-defense counterparts in this regard; knowing how wasteful and inefficient sequestration would be at DoD, I have no doubt the same is true at other departments and agencies as well.

Remind them that sequestration's impact on our domestic budget will cause further long-term damage to our defense – because the strength of our nation depends on the strength of our economy, and a strong military needs strong schools to provide the best people, strong businesses to provide the best weapons and equipment, and strong science and research sectors to provide the best new innovations and technologies.

Remind them that we can't keep kicking this can down the road. The more we prolong tough decisions, the more difficult and more costly they will be later on.

VI. CONCLUSION

The men and women of the Department of Defense are counting on Congress to help assure the strength of our military and American global leadership at a time of great change in the world.

We must reverse the decline in defense budgets to execute our strategy and fund a modern, ready, leaner force in a balanced way. We must seize the opportunity to enact necessary reforms in how we do business. And we must bring an end to the threat sequestration poses to the future of our force and American credibility around the world.

As you evaluate the President's budget submission, I encourage you and your colleagues to keep it in perspective.

In the years since the President's Fiscal Year 2012 budget request – the benchmark for cuts prescribed under the 2011 Budget Control Act – DoD's 10-year budget projections have absorbed more than $750 billion in cuts, or more than three-quarters of the trillion-dollar cuts that would be required should sequestration be allowed to run its course. And while some claim this is our biggest budget ever, the fact is, as a share of total federal spending, DoD's Fiscal Year 2016 budget is at a near-historic low – representing about 14 percent of total federal discretionary and non-discretionary outlays. DoD's total budget remains more than $100 billion below what it was at the height of the wars in Iraq and Afghanistan.

I think we can all agree that the world in 2014 was even more complicated than we could have foreseen. Given today's security environment – which has over 200,000 American servicemembers stationed in over 130 countries conducting nearly 60 named operations – our proposed increase in defense spending over last year's budget is a responsible, prudent approach.

Some of you may recall how, in 1991, after America's Cold War victory and amid doubts about America's engagement with the world and calls for a bigger domestic peace dividend, a bipartisan group in Congress stepped forward to help shape America' global leadership and make long-term decisions from which we continue to benefit.

Senators Sam Nunn and Dick Lugar helped craft, pass, and pay for the small Cooperative Threat Reduction Program that allowed the United States and DoD to provide the funding and expertise to help former Soviet states decommission their nuclear, biological, and chemical weapon stockpiles.

The Nunn-Lugar program was initially opposed abroad, and there were also doubts at the Pentagon about whether we could implement it without losing track of funding. I know. I helped lead the program in its early years. But with slow and diligent effort by American defense officials, the Congress, and our foreign partners, it worked.

It helped prevent weapons of mass destruction from falling into the wrong hands. It helped establish a pattern of international cooperation and global norms in the post-Cold War international order. And, in the light of the current instability in Ukraine, it might have staved off several variants of nuclear disaster.

But it also set an important precedent for our work on this budget and in the years ahead. It shows what Congressional conviction – especially when it is bipartisan – can accomplish in foreign policy. It shows the value of foresight and planning for an uncertain future. And it shows how spending a relatively few dollars today can generate huge value down the line.

As the new Secretary of Defense, I hope it will be possible to again unite behind what our great nation should do to protect our people and make a better world, and provide our magnificent men and women of the Department of Defense – who make up the greatest fighting force the world has ever known – what they deserve.

Thank you.

#

Page Left Blank

Page Left Blank